The Red Line

Also by Betsy Sholl

Changing Faces (1974)
Appalachian Winter (1978)
Rooms Overhead (1986)

The Red Line

BETSY SHOLL

University of Pittsburgh Press

Pittsburgh • London

The publication of this book is supported by grants from the National Endowment for the Arts in Washington, D.C., a Federal agency, and the Pennsylvania Council on the Arts.

Published by the University of Pittsburgh Press, Pittsburgh, Pa. 15260
Copyright © 1992, Betsy Sholl
All rights reserved
Manufactured in the United States of America
Printed on acid-free paper

This book is the winner of the 1991 Associated Writing Programs' award series in poetry. Associated Writing Programs, a national organization serving over 150 colleges and universities, has its headquarters at Old Dominion University, Norfolk, Va. 23508.

Library of Congress Cataloging-in-Publication Data

Sholl, Betsy.
    The red line / Betsy Sholl.
       p.   cm.—(Pitt poetry series)
      ISBN 0-8229-3722-0 (alk. paper).—ISBN 0-8229-5482-6 (pbk. : alk. paper)
      I. Title. II. Series.
    PS3569.H574R4   1992
    811'.54—dc20   92-50197
                                      CIP

A CIP catalogue record for this book is available from the British Library. Eurospan, London

The author and publisher wish to express their grateful acknowledgment to the following publications in which some of these poems first appeared: *Beloit Poetry Journal* ("Dawn," "*Real Faux Pearls*," "A Small Patch of Ice"); *Cafe Review* ("Bird Lady," "The Y"); *Field* ("Joining the Circus," "Pick a Card," "Three Deaths"); *5 AM* ("Midnight Vapor Light Breakdown," "Sex Ed"); *Graham House Review* ("Something to Say"); *Hanging Loose* ("The Hospital State"); *Ploughshares* ("The Red Line," "Three Wishes"); *Poetry Miscellany* ("Lights Out"); *Sojourner, The Women's Forum* ("Old Birds," "You Figure it Out") and *West Branch* ("The Argument, 1973," "The Feel," "Outside the Depot," formerly "What the Moon Won't Let Me Forget," "Thinking of You, Hiroshima").

"A Girl Named Spring" first appeared in the *Cimarron Review* and is reprinted here with permission of the Board of Regents for Oklahoma State University, holders of the copyright.

"The Coat" is reprinted from *The Massachusetts Review*, © 1991, The Massachussetts Review, Inc.

"The World Snow Posits," "Drifting Through This Pious Town," and "Forget Your Life" appeared in *The Eloquent Edge*, published in 1990, by Acadia Publishing Company of Bar Harbor, Maine; and appear with permission of the publisher.

Several of these poems appeared in the chapbook, *Pick a Card*, 1991 winner of the Maine Arts Commission chapbook competition, published by Coyote/ Bark Publications.

Lyrics from "The Blues Is a Thief" appear with the permission of the author, David Sholl, © Safe Sax Music (BMI).

Special thanks to Mark Cox, Lynda Hull, Susan Mitchell, and David Wojahn.

for Doug

I want to believe that the forces above us,
Engaged in doings we cannot imitate,
Touch our cheeks and our hair sometimes
And feel in themselves this poor flesh and blood.

—Czeslaw Milosz

Contents

1

Real Faux Pearls

the announcer promises, and we snicker:
a real falsehood with its own 800 number
sponsoring the evening news—bizarre
as those fast-talking men from childhood's low

transmission channels, who used to peel, dice,
shred—anything in thirty seconds, with
a one time only, while they last, magic
kitchen device. Those afternoons, mother

at work, we'd rearrange her diamonds and
pearls, opals, aquamarines. We knew where
each one came from, and which would be ours when
she died—as if that's the price. And how else

to appraise grandmother's humongous ring,
but by hours of laundry taken in,
steps paced in the shoe store, by the music
and books she didn't have, not to mention

the mines back then. Now in a crusted leather
case on my dresser that ring sits glowering
and silent, like grandfather refusing
to lift his legs while she feels under the sofa,

sticks her hands in crevices between cushions,
her tears magnified by thick lenses
until finally she catches its gleam
in a tangle of hair stuck to the broom.

Those old days, miners went down before sunrise,
came up after dark. A man would be sent
in alone to test the air because mules
were expensive. Now, they could wear masks,

make black lung a thing of the past, but they don't.
And as if they need an edge to keep from getting
claustrophobic, they even carry butane
lighters in their pockets as they lie

on their backs rattling through the dark,
straight down. On Sundays, the same men sit
in church, shoulders hunched, faces pale as feet,
necks in tight collars—grown men at the altar

dropping pearls from their eyes for a lost friend,
a bad marriage—*faux* maybe, Sunday pearls,
because it takes a long time to really
mean it when you say you'll change, to really

see how false things are, like my own precious
hide, for instance, the way I was taught to
hold back, contain myself, cast nothing before
swine, and see swine everywhere. A pearl

could be somebody's eyes, it's possible,
a real one at least—the wide stunned eyes of
a young diver caught in a rock chamber. Coal
comes from lungs. You can see along the tracks,

they walk stooped and wheezing, up the hill to
the clinic—thin lungless men, never as
old as they look. If I think this hard enough,
what will be precious to me? If I shut

my eyes, make myself dark and still, here,
where light through a green glass lily, a red flame,
falls onto white cloth, what will I find—down
on my knees among this coughing, these tears?

Thinking of You, Hiroshima

Champagne goes straight to my head
so I hear beneath neat family hedges and lawns,
the dresses and ties we wear to dignify my 40th birthday,
how the trees with their long roots catch the city's throb
to release it above us in a dark sway. Jazzed up on the sky's
electric glare, I'm slow dancing with the whole night,
sweet gone music of willows. The patio

steadies my heels, but its cracks rise up and taunt
till I can't resist the shatter, a little break
in the perfect fit of things, a screech
to alleviate the silver strings emanating from the house.
No one follows me into the woods where I used to hide
as a kid, imagining a shadowy girl I never knew,
who knew shadowy things I couldn't imagine.

The party's relieved to glide around me, sisters
tracing each other's smiles, charming and calm,
brothers clustered, erupting in laughter. All these
beautiful people—no one wrings hands or glares wild eyed.
No one's grown fat. No one rubs my thigh, or crumbles
to blow like the bridges that summer I was born.
Sweet gone Hiroshima, I can't help thinking
each time I come home, something's got to give.
I can't get down to the music playing at my roots.

Which is not this muted rush of traffic's arteries
around the city, parts so barren I want to slam myself
into a tree. And not this little clink of ice in our glasses,
the murmur of voices that don't rise when they're angry
but fall, clenched and slow.

This can't be what they were saving the world for.
Something didn't grow as it should have, loose and generous,
like the tip ends of leaves barely distinguishing themselves
from air. There was a girl I didn't know, born the same day
as me, who was supposed to move as I move, root to my branches,
as mine would be root to her. I used to stand on the shore
singing to her on hers singing to me.

Something was stunted.
Lanterns clink on wires clenched to the trees.
One blink and her lids were fused to her eyes.
Sometimes I try to make myself see her
standing on a bridge whose far end is not visible
beyond the rise of its arc. When she turns to me
I try to say I am not alone with the darkness, lushed
and garrulous, listening to trees, trees leaning together
advanced, unbearably patient, like another race.

The Coat

I stare at the blue linoleum
while my mother grieves for her lost sister,
not dead, just more trashed than usual—
my aunt, I suddenly recall from years ago,
sunk to her knees on this floor

begging my uncle to go to the Red Lion
for another bottle of Scotch, then going
herself, in high heels, on the cindery
shoulder of the road, tear streaks through powder
on her face, wearing a real leopard coat.

She came back, pine needles and leaves stuck
to her shoes, cradling the bottle, baby-
talking to my mother who chopped onions
and didn't look up, my uncle who stared at
the news. *What's going on?* I must have asked

and nobody answered, so I turned it
over in my mind, the swirls in that coat,
the streaks on her face, her red plastic jangle
of bracelets, till once, in college, I woke
with a headache, nauseous, and thought: leaning

from arm to arm, into those huge faces,
Oh, that's who I was last night. Now I hear
that at a barbecue in Shore Acres,
beside those black glassy lagoons, she got
so drunk she called my mother *Joan, Joan,*

the name of her daughter, poked slurred advice
into my mother's chest, grabbed her as she
tried to pull away, so they both nearly
fell into the hot grill. I can imagine
my mother's face, patient, sad, turned slightly,

too careful to actually say, *Aren't you*
ashamed? My aunt spills her drink on the grill,
laughs—what the hell—lights the wrong end of
a cigarette, and in the sudden stench
and flare, I picture their two faces

like different answers to the same question,
as if for years each thought—if *she* is right,
then *I* am terribly wrong, each looking
at herself in the other's mirror. What was
the question? My mother doesn't remember.

It was my aunt who described how their father
would come home glowering, not speak for days,
not raise his voice, or touch them. Just glare
till their skin felt like sieves. My mother learned
to stare off to the side, closed in her own thoughts,

while my aunt kept looking, asking, *What did*
I do? with that way she jiggles her head,
as if listening so hard something has to
explode. Maybe that's it. I've seen her fling
her arms as she talks, so liquor splashes

against the wall. She gets louder as night
goes on, not wanting to know when it might
start again—the silence, perhaps, the glare.
I've seen a table slip out from under her,
her clatter against a wall, knocking down

pictures. *Who did that?* she wags her head,
blaming a table or rug, then the faces
pointing toward her. And maybe she's right—
how can a family let just one person
wear all the scars? I didn't live with glares,

but with such tight, restrained voices,
plenty of times I've put on that coat
the color of sunlight on Scotch, its burning
swirl of black eyes. I've put on the fear
as evening begins to teeter and slide,

that ash on the tip of a cigarette
bobbing in somebody's mouth, ash on the grill
she knocks over, kicks across the white
pebbled ground. *You all right?* they rush up,
and I feel skinless too in their hands,

tightening to steady her as she blurs from
face to face, trying to decide the answer—
whether to throw back her head and roar,
or just close her eyes and slip through them,
their stupid miserable questions.

The Distinct Call of the Alligator

The first time I flew over Florida I was amazed
by all the green, and the blue crimp of waves
up and down the shore like a living relief map
only God could see wholly. Something about
the palm trees made me feel all I'd been taught
was true, it was possible to do something right.
Those elegant birds with long slender legs,
all those pelicans gliding smooth as TV ads,
made me want to reach into myself with both hands
and pull up my heart.

                But if I gave it to you,
you'd probably screw up your face as you always did
over turkey innards, and probably still do,
even in this strange Novemberless Florida,
this Florida where you no longer drive at night,
no longer see the stars, where you have more
doctors than days in the week, which is not
what they discovered it for.

                This morning I set out
with a spiral notebook and blank tape to recover
my youth. I want my childhood, which you've saved
in a drawer under yellow linen monogrammed
with strange initials. I want something to prove
I wasn't adopted, am not a changeling whose thoughts
got crossed between a forgotten language
and the one you taught which is very stiff.

You claim you don't live in the past,
but it's written all over your face that the past
lives in you. And if you won't tell me
what you remember of your first lie, how can I ask
what entered your mind the moment I was conceived?

Or why, for so many years, you turned my name into
this persistent bird cry, which you repeated again
last night just because I let a map fly out the window
and slap against the windshield of another car.

Ah Florida, Florida. Not its beautiful name,
not its red birds singing all night in the gardenia,
not its oranges glowing in branches over smudge pots,
nor its white egrets perfectly balanced on one leg
can repair this visit. You want to be good,
I want to be honest. All we know to do is deny
each other, as if out of some deep terror
in the blood, some swampy place where creatures live
half in, half out of the water, creatures
with powerful jaws and very sly smiles
we had matching purses made out of once.

The Y

for Carolyn Chute

Unlike St. Peter who sank when he looked down,
this guy's bent, pumping like mad, intent on
keeping speed over the shifting amoebic shapes
he probably can't even see. He's probably not
even thinking that besides the exercise bike,
the hard floor, there's another reality
pool water swirls on the plate glass.

But the gray-haired woman chuckling beside me
sees it—how he pedals yet gets no closer
to these eleven year olds lined up on the pool's
edge, their gently emerging torsos and thighs.
The guard eyes her collection of bags, and I'm
trying to imagine myself ten years from now
wandering in here the Tuesday before Thanksgiving
watching children I have no connection to.

Why would a woman do this? Why would she
get on a bus, let the road flatten everything
behind her, then step off somewhere in Maine,
one of those flat-roofed cinder block stations,
enter a coffee shop and ask for the Y?

My mother used to ask why I collected
such people. Why I had to think so much,
couldn't stick to my job, why I had to ride my bike
down to the piers to watch the water hypnotizing itself.
She'd imagine me indigent, or married to a used car
dealer who tampers with the mileage.

But maybe you can't roll back
anything, you can't undo what was done to you
and shouldn't even try. Maybe it's all recycled
pool water, past and future at the same time,
and *now* is a shimmering lesson
some kids find hard to trust, while others
grow fluent as eels, expecting the water to love them.
Maybe we got worked up, Mother, over the wrong stuff.

Is it so unreasonable
to want to sit in this steamy balcony
watching the miraculous children
hesitate and lunge? I want to ask
what's in her bags—objects distilled from a dream
it is urgent to keep wherever she goes?

Etiquette tells me, be quiet.
But she's kind enough to shake her head and
make the joke with me, how the man pedals nowhere so fast,
while we lean on the bleachers' stiff resilience,
among the echoes of children immersed in their schooling,
little parables of survival.

A Girl Named Spring

The only calm here is the trees, waiting
since childhood, where they never sighed
impatiently as I transposed the numbers
backward onto my work sheet, never snatched it
from my hands to do it right. Maple, mimosa,
razor-leafed Japanese elms, japonica—names
written in a tiny notebook hidden under the bed
along with dark angry words—

                          which must have
something to do with how I got from that childhood
to this girl, with a bunch of kids ditching school.
Hair dry from too much bleach and perm, thick
lipstick, black around her eyes, it's hard for her
to light a cigarette and walk at the same time
in high heels, a tight skirt, the wind.
The guys go loping off. Her girlfriend hesitates

then quick steps after them, leaving this one
alone with the match in rain. Fuck it, she mutters.
Then calls out, Wait, hobbling behind them.
And I remember something like that, hobbling
after my sister in wooden shoes on Halloween,
always having to be a Dutch girl or Bo-peep,
never a werewolf or witch. I was allowed out
one hour with my sister before dark.

                              So maybe
inside this girl who was given more darkness
than she wanted, left alone in it, allowed to become
a little whore—maybe inside of her is a soft creature,
tender and skittish as her name, *Bambi*. And maybe
you could talk it out to the edge of a clearing,
if you were patient and calm, the way I imagine
they talked her sister off the bridge,

14

a jumpsuited guy stretching his hand slowly,
no sudden moves, a flat voice telling her
what she didn't know, how to step back from the edge,
easy does it, one slick metal stair at a time. Nobody's
going to hurt you, it's OK—though her name is *Spring*
and she's got a long way to go starting from inside that van
with the word rescue written backward across its hood,
its windshield a crazed reflection of bare limbs.

Dawn

At the day camp years ago where we drove
from the projects to an outlying municipal park,
the trees were so lush, the kids didn't know
what to do with that soft filtered light,
so unlike raw sun blasting the sidewalks.
They'd glare, spin out a wisecracking jive,

or hide their faces against a trunk, gouging
the bark. One of the tough girls, 8 years old,
high octane mouth, called me *Kotex breath*
then flopped in my lap. Sweat made her dark skin
iridescent. See them birds? she asked, leaning back.
She went to the country once, on a bus, to visit

her grandfather and he had all kinds of birds,
craziest racket you ever heard. We watched a few
fuss in and out of the leaves, catching light
on their wings, light making everything its own color,
so we couldn't tell bird wing from jiggling leaf,
and I totally believed we were all connected. Only

I wasn't thinking just then about trash in the street,
or crumbling blacktop, or what it's like to climb
twelve flights in the dark through that pissy smell,
the sound of feet rushing up behind you.
That afternoon while the top branches caught
some barely translatable breeze, I couldn't answer

when all this poured out and she put it to me—
how come, how come? Instead I traced letters
on her back for her to guess, this little girl
who the next day didn't show, and when she did
wouldn't speak to me, so I don't know what
to say about the hardness she came to,

whether it was wrong or right, I just remember
her back shaking in spasms as she threw those
rocks, making the water fly up and shine a minute
before it disappeared, her back which had jerked
itself away from me, as if to say—You are useless,
you don't know, you don't know a thing.

Lights Out

The first time I saw them they were sitting
on folding chairs against the basement wall of a church
that hadn't changed the pictures in fifty years—
same tepid Christ, same pale shadowless children.
Wooden floors, middle of the week. Boy Scouts,
or annual Lion's charity show—some civic duty
repetition grinds into gibberish. I conjured
a sullen thought: What we love too easily betrays us.
The moon taught me this, that coffee can lid
I tacked to the wall because the real one depressed me.
I didn't love it, but its fullness, and so had to
suffer continual loss, hearing the sound of its gears
shifting across the sky. I tried not to think:
It's the same sickness my neighbor must have,
stepping addled out of the all-night adult movies,
hands in his pockets sifting through coins of inadequacy,
change from whatever he bought, which was already gone
when he cut the lights and turned into the drive,
gone as snow falling on water, gone as the rabbit
that made the dogs bark, as the smell of sex
is long gone from his wife.

~

The first time I saw the new moon with the old
in its arms, someone else's sorrow fingered my eyes
till they wouldn't shut. I was going to those neighbors
with a plastic jug to buy fresh milk from their cow.
Stars in the branches cross-hatching the drive,
a door slamming. Pulling out, his car threw gravel
against my legs and I actually saw the whole moon,
though nearly all of it black, an absence so real
your life could cave in around it. She slid
to the floor holding the phone away from her ear
as a voice crackled her name, Mother. Then we were
on the steps, the weight of her sobs in my lap.

I tried not to jostle her broken nose, eye swollen shut.
It seemed that moon might suck me right into itself,
or it already had, because as the evening went on,
as we waited on those steps for her daughter,
it was she who patted my hand murmuring,
"All right, dear, it's all right," as if
something bigger were rocking us both.

~

This must be an ode to pain, to my neighbor's
three returns, to all the sorrows of our lives
and the last long ache which is that none of them
transforms us enough. The last time she left,
I was standing in the shadow of a tree,
watching through red exhaust, though the way
headlights from her daughter's car illumined her
against the door, I might as well have been
catapulted into her swollen face. I could see
why she lingered, the whole dark house at her back,
her daughter yelling, "Just get in the car."
Almost anyone would have seen it, though what it was
is hard to say. Something sullen like:
Wherever she goes, she will carry the darkness
of that house inside her. But is it a curse?
Or is the unlit fullness of the moon something you
curl yourself around, something that makes you whole?

~

Did I say my neighbor lives with a tremor,
a perpetual nod, and even crouched in her doorway
sobbing as his car spins out, her head shakes
in runaway affirmation? Looking up, she calls it
a singing moon because its mouth has come into view.
He's split her lip. Her daughter's in the car

muttering, "Fool, fool." But she does what she has to:
stands on that porch trembling till her shoulders slump
and bitterness drops like gravel from her hands.
Black, hunched ridges in the distance divide what we know
from what's unimaginably beyond us. She stares
till she sees the cow go dry, twelve guinea hens
get knocked from the sky, sees him jerk the tractor
through fields till they stink with diesel
and he turns it over on its side cursing himself
voiceless. At the doorsill, praying God have mercy,
with her one good eye, she stands there knowing this
knowing this knowing.

The Hospital State

The smell of piss guides us down the halls,
strong aromatic to keep us scowling.
The doctor doesn't care how gracefully the blind boy
moves when allowed to walk in his preferred direction,
that is, backward to us: Just don't let him.
Make him go head-on, tripping over himself
because truth's not supposed to be pretty anymore.

Nevertheless, the hands of these spastic children
keep trying to effervesce, to lift off, chair and all—
grinning, nodding, drooling children who say *daaa daaa,*
meaning yes, in whatever language they speak
in this bald hospital where the gravity's all wrong.

Sometimes lining them up, tied to their green chairs,
my hands would laugh if I let them, just flap themselves
in huge guffaws, wanting to answer a question, any question,
like what drug would you have to take, what terrible
thoughts would you have to repeat for nine months
to produce a life so completely misconnected
it keeps jerking out of itself.

The doctor congratulates me after watching
an autistic girl yank out a patch of my hair.
From his office, over closed circuit TV
he seems to think we were trading pleasantries
in some dialect of Martian, her grabbing my hair,
my hand flying into her mouth.

In the worker's lounge, two orderlies
are out of their seats, fists jabbing the air
shouting yes YES
because—just seconds left—there's a steal,
a long pass, and a three point shot wins the game.

Bunched up in the doorway behind brooms
three smiling moon faces with almond eyes
try to understand this sudden burst of clarity.

No matter how far I drive from this place
I find I have left as collateral to a strange god
my right shoulder blade where the wing snapped off
at birth, and a certain piece of scalp that crawls
whenever I watch someone who perfectly fits,
as after a slam dunk, the guy comes back down
in slow-motion replay like a great heron folding
back exactly into himself, everything we wanted
to say. Take that.

Something to Say

Hyped up on caffeine and Thorazine
you tried to explain the jailbreak from Houston,
3 A.M. in my kitchen, pacing, exhaling.
Your favorite aunt, I sat on a backless stool,
wilted and limp, blown away

watching your eyes dart
as you tuned in channels from some snowy
galactic void, playing an on-off switch so fast
in your mind the screen enlarged itself
till the whole world was inside and you
were its hired prophet.

You rode the bus from Houston,
pulling smokes from your blond kinky hair,
radiating unease through the crowd—watch this guy,
don't mess around.

You had gotten incredibly strong—
half workout in a gym on doctor's advice,
half drumbeat of whatever you found to dance
through your veins, *to hide*

you explained, from the grinning baby
you were just then bugging your eyes out for,
when some inner stalactic voice began chanting
stab, stab. I never saw you again.

Cops picked you up in Austin. Stolen car,
sawed-off shotgun, couple of machetes.
Crouched on the floor, eyes darting, ready to
shoot out a squad of translucent nebuloid hit men—

you weren't expecting bluecoats, no that was all wrong.
You blinked, went along without resisting,
strangely relieved by their frisking hands.

For the broken immunities of your mind
they locked you up in a hospital, gave you pills
to make your feet drag, slur your speech.
The doctor is too earnest, you told your mother.

Pissing on couches for revenge
like some lobotomized grandmother, you cried—
Is this any way for the son of Stagmite Avenger?

Nights in the county jail taught you
how to use an overlooked hanger, how to count
between bed checks. Still, it was pure chance
that made the clothes rack strong enough.

"Let God take me now
before something worse does," you wrote
and I think you meant that.

So God give me something to say
stepping into my house near midnight,
feet wet from a slush puddle, and the phone's ringing
which'll be my sister again having to tell me
she can't make the pain go away.

Outside the Depot

I loved the way it felt once, practically invincible,
moving door to door, signing up people to vote, as if those men
idling in cars with guns at the vent windows were just there
for background effect. They were on us a whole day
before this kid pointed them out and said, "Fear's useless.
They can't beat you into somebody you don't know." It was just
fact to him, walking down the road. He was 16, he'd cut school
to be there, said he'd worry about that after we left.

We all worried the night our bus left town,
a full moon bouncing through the trees like a dot along
the words of a song. Stomachs tightened, our words
thinned to nothing when we saw the cars outside the depot,
the kids turning their perfect dark faces away from us
to slip through the crowd as if there were still time
to surround themselves with friends in some part of town
those men wouldn't go.

Who can say anything sane about these moments?
Weeks later I got the clipping and sat up in bed
thinking the trees along the road were clearer to me
than exactly what they did to his face.
I read *tire iron,* and *chains.* Some must have held,
while others pummeled and kicked.

He told me they sang. In the road they lay,
saying the good words to themselves like three men
in an empty hall hearing love songs meant for a crowd.
Half a block from the station, they had walked right into it—
the car, the drive down some dark road, blindfolded and tied,
bouncing in ruts. They had to listen to that slow vicious snarl
learned from dogs. It hurt. Then the water stilled
and still they were there, the moon lingering in rain puddles
beside their cheeks. They didn't move all night, just sang.
Even laughed, he told me. I didn't know how to write back.

The Argument, 1973

Top of the stairs, Times Square Station, a man reels
toward me, asks for a cigarette, and because I'm proving
New Yorkers aren't heartless, I tell him—Just keep the pack.
But he's stepping back, shaking his head, saying
I need them worse than him, what with it being
five o'clock, the baby howling, stroller springing open
in my hands. He lights one and puts it in my mouth,
takes another for himself, tucks the rest
back into my pocket.

As if I couldn't live off that a long time,
the wet filter between my lips, my mother speechless,
he goes even further, grabs me just as I trip
on the top step with a crowd pushing from behind,
so I see how demographics are crap. You just jump tracks
and become something else. I don't know why I'm sobbing.
He's promising to keep me crammed up against him
as long as I need to shake. As long as I want to
bore my head into his grungy tweed not caring
if it does cost me my wallet or crabs or whatever—
he's willing to thumb the snot off my face
and inebriate my hair, saying—It's all right, girl,
you'll make it.

Though I no longer know what *it* is,
or where we're going, my mother and I,
on the same train, the jab and slit of leather seats,
the bare feet of my son like pale flowers
drawing the gaze of wary travelers. She leans over
to tell me something that gets lost in the window's
lurid comment on our faces.—You never know,
is all I hear as the car lurches and my kid smears
two wet fingers around the dark bruise,
a man's swollen cheek, you never know.

Midnight Vapor Light Breakdown

This ladies' room fluorescence will not be ignored,
this pure malicious glare guessing my age,
not even asking for money. It tells me

I'm the only white person in the club, and it's
a shame I'm so pasty and unadorned, so nearly fog
only pity can make a move this evening, a bad light

to be left in. Two dimes, no phone book, and my car
broken down. Walking out alone, I am myself a beam
in everyone's eye, calling attention to something no one

leaning against the Rainbow Lounge intended this evening.
A sort of clarity like when the sun fires factory windows and
suddenly blind, it's midnight standing outside my useless car,

this guy running his hand down my arm. What's happening, Babe?
The whole street turns its brights on us, tells him to
hot-wire something. He leans back, testing my arm

to see if it's genuine leather, while I explain whatever
comes to mind, how I read this morning that skin's
all we've got to keep us from oozing out of ourselves,

oozing like this weird light on the faces gathering around,
the sound of glass breaking, a few chuckles I can't
translate into friendly. He's got a diamond in his nose.

He can run this scene on any speed he wants, which
right now is very slow, sliding into my car, jiggling
his head a little like he's fine tuning the pedals and dials

into a jazz I didn't know they could make.
All the while he's looking at me, no smile, looking
through me to that narrow doorway beside the bar where

stairs rise unlit and steep, which I could climb, I think,
real slow. Drive you wild. Only just then the engine
kicks in, like I'm definitely not running this show.

He eases out from the wheel. A little drum roll
on the hood, and his face so close to mine he barely
whispers. Keep revving it, Babe. Then I'm gone

under the el's fractured light, the neon rainbow shorting
out behind an ambulance taking the corner on two wheels,
which I'd like to believe is a baby wanting

to be born. I'm saying, the way he looked at me—
it was summer, our clothes were thin. I could
have gone, up those stairs with him.

Sex Ed

Well-dressed, demure, jammed into those
politely arranged desks, it's hard to be
serious, but we are. No one even parts lips
to acknowledge what used to drive us crazy
in the back seats of cars, what kept us up
half the night reliving the last slow dance,
girl on her toes, guy bent at the knees
to press in against her.

The instructors speak precisely about
the importance of our children knowing the facts,
so surely none of us in our high heels and
neck ties is going to admit how our first mistakes
have suddenly blossomed so tender and lovely
we've been forgiven a thousand times,
a thousand times forgiven and repeated ourselves.

But fingering the graffiti on this desk,
I remember being braille to you, being read
like a steamy novel, and how those lessons
stayed with us, practical as driver's ed, those hours
of simulation behind the wheel of a parked car.
The truth is I don't regret having studied with you
though I do feel inarticulate, like an athlete
asked to speak in a room of kids, who has nothing
to say except, "practice, practice."

Once our daughter watched the cat in heat
yowl and slither across the floor, and without
looking up asked, would that happen to her. Sometimes
it isn't shame that makes us speechless. It's not
regret that makes me linger at the curb watching
her toss back her yellow hair and yank open
the heavy doors to school.

"The Blues Is a Thief"

—David Sholl

The singer rasps, *the blues is a thief,* and the sax has
all kinds of sultry things to say. *Doin damage to myself,*
you know I'm drinkin all the time. Across the street
a woman leans against a factory wall, open blouse,

short skirt. She makes that cigarette look tough,
like my first one, and the friend who taught me,
always two steps ahead, on some edge, turning
to ask—Are you coming, or what? I don't know

why I listened but I did. Blues, booze, guys. *Trashed*
my soul, made my life a mess. The woman paces now,
tapping her thigh, waiting for the men who cruise
to slow down and call. Once on a bridge

my friend dared me to jump, flat out defy
my fear. I wasn't thinking just then how the river
snatched every bottle we drained, how it swirled
out of sight, currents we couldn't see

sucking our empties under. I was nothing to them,
a kid to roll, another chick like the one across
the street, who doesn't know how far the bottom can drop.
Before I lost it, or thought I did, my life flashed

in odd pieces—drawers yanked out, scarves dangling,
my mother in a green wool skirt turning to speak.
I woke on the bank throwing up, the whole scene
strangely lit—slash of light across factory brick,

curb at my cheek flecked with silver, every grass blade
sharpened—the edge you come to, hold for a while.
What you do to get it back—Lord, that's what the blues
are about. A new song inside, *You're still tryin to land me,*

but, see, I'm already there, which I knew briefly
that afternoon I stepped into traffic, left my friend
at the crosswalk saying swear, swear you won't tell.
The truth is I always did what she said,

and even that time told no one, didn't speak of it
for years, till I began to think it was a dream,
maybe nothing was true. *Feelin kind of worthless,*
like my life ain't worth a dime, and who doesn't

know that tune? My friend, the last night I saw her,
was too drunk to stand. I said, Girl, there were times
I could have killed you. She just stared straight ahead,
let the smoke out both sides of her mouth. And that's where

I left her—until tonight, waiting to get in this bar
because I like the boozy music, its sexy jive,
though I know where it can lead. Across the street,
a washed-out hooker's trying to make this factory district

sultry Bogart. I could go over, bum a cigarette off her.
She'd cup her hands to my face, match flaring between us.
Thanks, I'd say, as she leans against the wall, exhaling,
eyes closed, skirt riding up. Sure, Bitch, any time, any time.

A Small Patch of Ice

If I told you we could see nail polish stopping
a run in one skater's tights, a safety pin
in a zipper, that their patch of ice was the size
of my kitchen, no room to leap or spin—you might
agree with my daughter hissing fiercely, *Let's go.*
All they do is circle to tinny music, then stop
in a flourish of shaved ice. But the little mist
that makes reminds me of the gray flickering light
in those films where you come to care about
a balding aerialist, a clown weeping back stage,
the way they'll talk later in their van, in French
or Italian, with subtitles, about despair.

Maybe that's why I linger. Or is it the smell
of popcorn and cotton candy mixed with machine oil
from a hand-pushed Zamboni—the smell of boardwalks
from childhood, neck-jerk rides, tiered rows of teacups
you toss quarters into, those wiry barkers with burnt
cheekbones, voices snatching at your back—Hey, girl
in pink shorts. So we stay to the end.
Then while I scrape a thin crust of ice off
the windshield, my daughter says: *If you can't
do it right, you shouldn't do it at all.*
She's just seen the Olympics on TV and
doesn't like to think how far from grace things

can fall, or how most of us just circle and trudge,
like these skaters, in boots and jeans now, lugging
the heavy ice frame, the clunky machines out to
the U-Haul behind their van. Soon they'll doze,
or bitch, or razz each other about who gets the seat
by the wheel well. Someone will let out a long sigh
settling in by the window, longing for what
we call "the real thing"—the kind of ice you need
to work out fast and hard. In those movies, sometimes

the hard pressure of facing just how far we are
from our dreams, turns someone kinky and wise,
fills the screen with pungent images we remember

for years—the sweep of birds across a square,
clown suit hanging on a line. I'm telling you this
because my daughter doesn't want to hear it.
She doesn't want to know those boardwalks
were full of legless men, I guess from the war,
and one leaned toward me, an anchor tattooed
on his arm where his rolled up sleeve cradled
a pack of smokes. A stub of a man, with apish arms,
he jiggled a cigarette in my face, the way someone
does with a bone to make a dog come. *Girlie,*
he whispered, as I ran off, and what good would it do
to tell my daughter there's grace in falling too,

in that guy starting after me on his crutches
with huge strides like an ungainly bird that might
actually take off, or the way he threw back
his head and laughed—so loud I still see him
on those thin stilts in the middle of the boardwalk
flustering parents so they grab their kids
and step wide around him. I was twelve then,
the age my daughter is now, and maybe it isn't
cruel to believe you'll never get so wounded
or shoddy. Maybe to grow at all we have to
pretend they have nothing to do with us,
these dark pleasures, this dinky patch of ice.

You Figure It Out

Behind me the sunken face of a woman
is telling her kid sit down, shut up, don't
touch, I'm gonna kick your butt, while the kid
makes leftover filters speed up and brake
around the rim of an ashtray. I can't look.

Though the way she lifts her hand to him,
the way her mouth says *don't* even when it's
shut, is played out on my face in the bus
station window just as that silver hulk
pulls in and docks. I pop a pill

so I'm pale and luminous and can watch
without flinching because whatever they
can do to a body they can do to you.
Like last night some jerk getting kicked
till he had no face and I screamed *police*

because I was not hard enough. I wanted
to go home, only just then I couldn't
think where that was. Now the driver's flipping
his giant Rolodex on the bus forehead
through Providence, Hartford, New York. The woman's

confused, picks up her bashed in suitcase, bangs
the kid on each step till he starts to howl.
Next she'll be calling him *brat, trash,* gouging
a wad of used gum from his mouth. She'll jerk
him into the seat so his neck half snaps.

A whole childhood like that, and he'll end up
with me watching this battered bitch face
in the sky rise pocked and orange over
a little plaza of flat-roofed stores that'll
dry clean you in 24. Eyes sunken

from midnight's throaty deejay speed-rapping
desire. X-ray ears to pick up
the chipped rim of a woman's voice scratching
across her kid's back. I'd get totally
scrambled. My old lady would say, Don't let

me see you like this again, or Who the hell
do you think you are? Damned if I know.
But I can tease a street, or walk it brisk
if I want, alone, like I got someplace
to go. And now, most any city, I find

myself down at the docks watching water
break up whatever light happens to fall.
Whoever's out there moves in like every slow
song he ever heard is turning its weird speed
in his gut. Wants to touch something

Mama can't slap away. Wants to need me
till I can't resist. Pours his voice in my ear,
thick like he swallowed his tongue. To which I'd
reply—Only, hey—what is it a dog says,
when it throws back its head and doesn't stop?

Soup Kitchen

Ginny at a table of young men belly dancing
their tattoos: gray hair in braids circling her head,
and maybe it's the way they can't make her flinch
that finally soothes them. Maybe the way she
speaks with a *you* that is intimate, gets through
their skulls, and that's why they ask almost sweetly
for rags to clean the mess they've made,

which when I come back is a huge clump of wet napkins
resembling puke and a lot of talk about outer space
inside their heads, with Ginny saying *grow up,*
straight into their guffaws, not like my mother's
clenched teeth hissing that things are hard and it's
not fair, the way we spill our milk night after night.
Out of an old plastic bag she pulls a gull feather

and weaves it through a hole in her sweater.
Evolution, she muses, telling me that down under
the bridge by the ferry, on a hot day she went wading
and saw dragonflies more delicate than any lace
I'm likely to wear, bluer than that blouse over there
across the room. Something planned that, she says,
tapping the vein inside her wrist. She fingers

the embroidery on my blouse, which I got
down the block, used, three bucks, I say, and wonder
if the woman who owned it is here, if she sold it
the way heavier ones sell blood, to wire their veins
hot with liquor. One of the mouthier girls
from two tables away yells—Hey, gimme that shirt.
That's how it is these days, Ginny shakes her head—

as if a little gentleness would kill them. I wonder
through what kinds of gentle and killing she's passed,
under bridges, in train yards. Are there other time zones

where she's had children? But the rule is: don't ask,
don't make her look down and shred her napkin.
Just take what she's willing to give tonight,
which is how she discovered secrets once in a hidden file

her bosses warned her to overlook. They walked toward her.
She could smell the metal of the gun. And then—
she's looking away, fumbling in her purse
for a pair of multicolored mittens she knit by rote
in the darkness of boxcars. She holds them up to the light,
little *x*'s on the thumbs so like my mother's, which she'd
pull out, start over, tightening her lips, while I sat

beside her asking why or what if, till she cried, Stop it,
and my face burned like this old guy Ginny nods to,
who looks plain drunk to me. That too, she says,
but he's got a terrible disease, and across the tables
she calls—God love you, to which he replies with a stiff
bow—Sweet lady, I cry out from my bed every night.
Yes you do, she tells him, and I believe her

since just then field lights come on in the next block
where school boys play soccer. That must be why,
returning her plate to the kitchen for seconds,
I forget I'm not her child. I pick up a piece
of crust pink with lipstick and put it into my mouth,
then stand there in that odd yellow light,
letting it soften.

2

The Red Line

Eight hours on my feet at Joe's Pizzeria and I know inside
this on-again, off-again red pulse of an arrow pointing
toward the tunnel my whole body wants to become.
Joe slams down the grate and we're gone, out on the street
where the neon craving of a train shudders into darkness
beside the art museum.

Waiting at midnight is one long flirtation,
watching the half-closed lids of a stranger slide from
the coins bulging at my thigh to the black funnel
I discovered one night with a six pack under the docks
when nothing the nuns ever said could answer the way
that boy's tongue hot-wired me.

Now I sometimes think any jerk on the street who can walk
two blocks without talking to himself is better than climbing
five flights alone, opening the door to a congress of roaches.
It's conceivable that I'll be nicer than I am tonight
tomorrow, wake up wanting exactly nothing, not feeling
every hair erect on my body.

Then I'll take the red line straight to its end
where oil and gas and dead fish yank all things into
perfect alignment. Wooden slats, stacked crates, winches,
pulleys, chains, water pouring out of fish houses, foaming
around pilings, water rumpled under rocking boats—
it'll be enough.

This time I'll believe that I am really inside
everything outside of me, like the nuns used to say.
Only to them it was all invisible, which was useless
down at the docks when those guys in tight jeans leaned
on the pilings. "You got what I want," they'd say. Then after
they got it, they forgot, and I was just another fishy thing

thinking how dumb it was to picture all those machines
suddenly in sync, coupled perfectly—lights, whistles, cash
registers springing at once, everyone in the street squinting,
mouths open like the mouths on primitive masks
where you can't tell ecstasy from pain, can't look away.
Now this smart-mouthed kid's eyeing me,

slinking around in the dark like he owns the place,
hustling the late-movie crowd. What's in it for him—
here in the midnight station where the drunk's already
waking to his turned-out pockets, and I am this hard core nun
with so many folds in my skirt he'll never get to a pocket,
never get to the one fold inside all skirts are gathered from.

I don't know why I can't turn away. He stands
on the edge of the platform spitting onto the third rail
wet strings gathered inside the darkness of his mouth
that become to me the single streaming window of a train
slowed down to separate frames—delayed
into a scorched rosary of light.

Pick a Card

I wonder if it still exists—Point Pleasant boardwalk,
Jenkin's Pavilion, old people rocking
deaf dumb and blind. Light bulbs flashing around
roulette wheels. If I blotted myself from the scene,
would the tide rush into the empty space? Or would there be
this jagged hole in the picture around which the water does its
break-and-be-healed, break-and-be-healed
routine, a photographic trick?

Couples strolling the long pier that night years ago
must have looked down and thought we were just kissing.
But that man's kiss split my lip, realigned my vision
into a tilting martini glass on the Rip Tide sign going
pink-green, pink-green, getting no place. I saw
how useless it was to try.

This morning when sleep finally settled down, folding itself
back out of me like wings, and I woke with heavy ankles,
a stiff neck, I was remembering against my will
that night summers and miles away, when I felt my arm
twist till I thought it would break, felt two fingers
force open my mouth . . .

To shake it off, I went to the community center
overlooking the harbor, was assigned the boy with the low IQ
who knows only one card trick, though he knows that well.
I settled in for a long afternoon of flash cards, Old Maid,
Go Fish. And watching that pale soft boy whose face could
not be dissuaded from shining, I imagined he materialized

from a mother walking home counting her tips, a father
in a ski mask flashing a knife. How far he must have
traveled to arrive at simple delight. He made me want
everything inside me that's been speeding on anger
to slow down and fall away, like this harbor after hours

when the cranes and dredging machines stop agitating
and water has a chance to be heard.

I can't possibly piece it all together, but I know that
for a long time after sitting with this unfinished boy
I'll be making lists of who to forgive. I'll be realizing
I don't know the first thing, after watching his mother
so tender with her fingers in his hair, hearing her tell me
there was not a better hand she was cheated out of.
The boy doesn't know much, but he can tell by her open face
that he's done something well, so he does it again.
Pick a card, any card.

144 Minden Street

I can still see him from down the block, my landlord, Charlie,
in sleeveless T-shirt—the kind with ribs we called
guinea tuxedos in high school, when Italians were all we had.
My old landlord in a shirt so yellow it's begging
his daughter-in-law to come take the laundry,

still stands on what's left of the front porch, cigar
in mouth, heaving gray sighs through the spring air.
He's been watching the purveyors of loss
take over the block, jabbering their unsavory tongues,
wearing glasses to further darken the streets which have

already daunted his daughter-in-law. She's elegant,
one of those whose car does not entrust itself
to our curb. I've never seen her, only bleached hair
through the tinted glass of a black car arriving bimonthly
to take the old man to dinner in the burbs, where presumably

emotion's recollected in tranquility,
not amplified, like the car doing *La Cucaracha*,
taking the corner on two wheels, which one night abruptly
docked itself under our house. It was cause for celebration
in the ghetto night—two guys saved by a hair and the beer

that relaxed them. But no number of dudes
saying—Be cool, old man, could stop Charlie
from hyperventilating over that hood jammed into our steps.
Such fate, he sighed, to survive Hitler and end up here.
If those fools had seen what I've seen, he started the next day.

And I should have said—What, Charlie, what?
Would they sober up, learn English? Are you telling me
you didn't see more than was good for you? Are you telling me
you've had anything good to say about life after Hitler?
Look, Charlie, at our fancy neighbor, in his handsome suit,

45

tumbling on the lawn with his sons: two guns
in leather holsters strapped to his chest and we know
he doesn't work for the cops. You'll be dead, Charlie,
before I can argue that, when the Feds move in, he'll up
the insurance and pay to have it burned—

the octagonal crib he's so proud of,
the enormous fish tank embedded in the wall—
all of it, Charlie, starting with oily rags in the hallway,
then chunks of roof glowing as they hit the street
and spatter like water balloons—everything we think

he's working so hard for in his own gangsterish way.
Charlie, you think I know nothing, but I'm going
to survive you. I'm going to stand here after you're gone,
leaning on the call box, looking at our new unpainted steps,
and resume this conversation, telling you—Don't leave.

You'll go nuts at your daughter-in-law's, won't last six months.
Here, at least you can go out strong, hold the floor, filibuster
on losing. Losing, Charlie, as if there's another way.
I'm watching the one tree on the block that survived the fire,
send its useless green tears all over the street,

wishing I had said to you then, in that piss-poor moment
so vivid in my mind: Don't leave us. There's nothing to climb,
the stairs are broken. That phone ringing on the third floor—
it's probably a wrong number, someone confusing us again
with the Boston Ballet.

Drifting Through This Pious Town

Look at this sweet drooling young man,
his by no means idiot face at the soup kitchen
emitting the most beatific smile
waiting to see what ring-strangled hand will lift a spoon
to his face—his face which he'll nuzzle into your side
as a way of loving since his arms don't work.
I'm telling you, don't fix him.

Myself, I don't ask to be relieved
of the way things misfire, the way you have to go to jail
to get warm and it's not as easy as it looks.
I do want to be loved, Lord, you know I do,
but if I was this dyslexic kid
filling out forms and misread *Dog* for *God,*
I'd wad it up too
and stomp out before some divine infestation
got into my clothes.

Everywhere I go,
from breakfast in the dark room under the sanctuary,
to the wharf if it's nice,
or the library on bad days where they let you
stay between reference and fiction with a newspaper
spread over your face—I meet people who think they are right
about everything that's wrong with the world.

Bird Lady

You think I don't work for the Feds? What do you know,
you're only here once a week and can't even get it straight
who takes black, who wants the sugars. I'm 91 years and 4 days.
If you don't believe it, I hope you live longer on less.
Just last week, with two lousy dimes and a used Handi Wipe
over the phone, I did a 9–1–1, and those chrome studs
have gunned through this street for the last time.

You like my glasses?
I wear them so you can't see nothing
but your self looking at me. That gets the little punks
with their stolen skateboards knocking up the sides
of the fountain. I flap bird shrieks in their faces,
and they drop my bags real quick.

I have mystical powers,
which the pigeons who picket this square reciting
Longfellow have revealed to me. When they single out
an individual to surround, namely myself, of which I have
photographic proof, they are making a statement of substance.

I sold antiques. I testified to Congress.
I could dump this bag of used crumbs right here
on your scuffed up floor, make them spell out your
pitiful future.

Any back room I want I enter. Swine, I tell them,
stupefied by your own desires. And they zip up,
they drop the dice. My face is contagious. I spit,
and they're out on the street, dazed, lice-raving birds,
stuck in their own throats.

And I want you to know, Miss-Dish-It-Out-So-Politely,
I did not always eat what was offered. I did not just take
what was put in my face, cooked in big pots, mashed down
for the toothless, of which I am not one,
but don't get so close.

24 Hours

Right now it's an old jughead in the laundromat
pulling levers on a candy machine like it's the slots,
wanting it to be moved by his buttonless coat's history
of eviction, how slandered even his breath is.

But the little packets inside hardly shake,
the coin return refuses to budge, so now he is pounding,
calling it Elsie, who won't open the frigging door,
who deserved that pop to the side of her head,
the way she's always complaining.

I finger the coins in my pocket
hoarded all week to stir these machines,
and wonder what ever happened to automats, those chrome
supersonic restaurants—no one between you and what you want—
shiny as finned cars, smoother than Sputnik, cooler than the cops
who any moment will saunter in here with their prerecorded voices,
Take it easy, Fella. Let's move it along.

All of us washing our clothes too close to midnight,
thinking to anyone else they look like rags,
feeling the rain outside slosh down the steamy windows
and pretending we don't know we're inside some thick churning
machine—we're a little awed by the way this guy slides
to his knees, the way in the end he's murmuring *please, please,*
among the vague rumble of drums, motors, freon
running through coils.

Fluorescence jiggles our eyes, seeps
the threads of our clothes till inside them our stomachs
curl, and the sluggish current of our blood wants to join in
crying *please, please,* groping for something to address,
a one-armed bandit to suddenly let loose, or that red-faced
priest out there trying to see what the commotion's about,

who might be persuaded to loosen his hands from
the invisible cuffs behind his back and run them down
this poor guy's head, saying whatever it takes
to make something move, *Elsie, Elsie, my God.*

Too Deep

Running out of the restaurant, my daughter and friends
elaborate their raucous wishes on the first star,
then leap over snowbanks, shoving each other into the car,
which their exuberance rattles and shakes
like the bus that summer I had twelve 8-year-old daughters,
at least from 9 to 5.

Riding from the city, they'd clap and stomp,
shiny faces lit from within, flashing bright recognitions,
or when someone was harsh, completely shutting down.
Once in a moment's bravado, Pamela, my favorite,
claimed: My daddy has three cars.

I winced, remembering how words like that come back.
But her friends were gentler than mine. Nobody said,
Oh yeah? Lemme see, nudging her with bike tires
till she was backed against a wall, or the other thing
they'd do to me, take off all together, turning once
to shout: You don't even have a daddy.

When the day camp had an overnight in the park, Pamela,
small body, big mouth, wormed into my sleeping bag,
shivering against me, the summer night unfamiliar
stripped of flashing lights and music, the reassuring walls
street voices made when she closed her eyes.

Look at the stars, I told her.
But she vice-gripped her wiry legs around me
because that was the problem, she said,
the stars were too deep.

Even if I had an answer to that,
the others would have pelted us with pine cones
and hissed, Shut up. So all night she huddled
against me while I lay on the knobby ground getting dizzy,

falling through the fathomless spaces she showed me,
where one minute you see a light and the next
you're not sure, it's so huge and far.

You can actually feel yourself shrinking.
Which may be why there is so much noise in this car.
And why the next morning there was no stopping that child.
She was all elbow, guffaws. Eyes practically spinning,
she jabbed and snatched at everyone in sight, mouth revved
like a deejay, terrified of silence—you know the feeling,
trying to talk yourself out of a jam you know is way too deep.

Old Birds

"It's a frigging bird," my son complains, and liking
the effect, repeats, "a frigging bird, man."
Then, "I'm gone," grabbing the ball, chucking the book
on the couch, thick Chaucer-to-Yeats, ending
with the weird Virginia Woolf, who takes,
he complains, eight pages to
leave a room.

            "Blithe Spirit!"—I remember
at his age, seeming more boy than bird, some fantasy
to conjure full of mist swirling under streetlights,
moon tongues licking water that was smooth and dark,
not at all what I knew at the shore where the surface
broke, one wave coming in, its huge torque dragging
the bottom till it toppled like a drunk over
whatever was trying to slip away.

                "Blithe Spirit!"—
I understood back then to be a shimmering self,
everything I wasn't—ethereal, whole,
the exact opposite of tangled legs and arms
in the back seat of a car, or the terrible desolation
I could explicate in detail, the way those cars
would peel out, leaving me in the driveway
under a smirking elm.

              So mist, moonlight
and this weird bird or fantasy boy pulled out of me
rapture without shadow or annoyance—
the way it was impossible, just
impossible with a real guy, when you feel like
you're nobody at all under his hands,
and you want to cry, want to have your spirit
not your body driving him wild, your spirit speaking
some shrill untamed tongueless bird everybody's
trying to get down.

        Instead, I leaned against streetlights
being worldly wise, blowing smoke like murky comic
balloons filled with words like *dreg* and *abyss*
let out in long exhalations. Birds—it took years
to forgive them, to let joy simply exist,
to let pigeons wade up to my bench
with those sweet sad songs stuck in their throats
and not shoo them away. It took me years
to get around to having a son
who pounds out his longing against a backboard
and doesn't keep score. He lets birds be birds.

The Feel

Windham Correctional Center, Poetry Workshop

We're stopped between two sets of bars,
where last week a woman in class told us
that frigging screw left her with a bunch of guys.
One, bending to tie his shoe, grazed her
breast with his teeth and bit. As she told this,
the men shifted under the table and I could

believe how they say it is in chapel,
the pews sticky with sex, men half deaf
with desire, so the minister's distinction
between spirit and flesh just spurts in and out,
and it would take a very loving God
to consider the strain on their faces prayer.

Now I'm saying, "Focus on where you are"—
as if you could eye solid brick and have
anything other than rage to break through.
But these guys write too much about moonlight
on water, love's easy rhymes, which they mean,
like the rest of us, until the pressure builds.

Then someone will show next week with scabs
where he's gouged his arms, or not show at all.
Once on a monitor in the guard station, I watched
a young man pull at the bars, try to squeeze himself
through. He'd step back, look it over, try again.
I thought he'd hurt himself. But the guys

at this table just shake their heads and say
everything here hurts, even sleep when you wake
to the static of guards on the radio, and can't
get back into that dreamy moon over open fields.
Can't find your smokes in the dark where you
left them, or drum out your roommate's farts,

so you pace the cold floor waiting for the long count
and bell. I thought of this last night reliving
the six miles between prison and home—
snow-blank fields, then the paper mill, enormous
and guarded, its inverted cloud so low and thick
I entered unprepared, couldn't pull off the road,

drove for blocks out of control, convinced
there was no way but to keep going, dangerous and
blind, until my husband's hands on my shoulders
woke me—so unlike the time in class a guy
shoved me down in the chair, then stepped back
blinking at his scuffed knuckles. All he wanted

was to serve me coffee, and the confusion
on his face was so raw, I had to turn
away, though I saw it again in the rearview
mirror of sleep, the crossed wires of that desire,
which would have been courtly any other place,
where touch isn't blown up into a photo

that makes your pores enormous. Now I have to
shake last night from my mind, how glad I was
to feel my husband's hands graze my thigh and
slowly gain intention, to feel desire
burn off sleep like fog, everything simple
and clear. But I can't talk about that here.

We've chalked twelve words on the board and now write
lines splicing that strange list into a poem,
so someone smells the moonlight, another calls
bare trees outside anorexic. Across from me
the other woman in class winces as I kick her
inadvertently again. I've been writing

of sun-licked bricks, the stun of light on snow
at four o'clock, till I catch myself in her eye
and every detail seems cruel—the weight of keys
in my pocket, the children in my wallet,
even the pineapple I brought, which creates
a taste nothing in here can satisfy. She shrugs,

and I think it's part kindness, part hard time
done with truth when she says, "I don't begrudge you
a thing." I look around the room at identical
blue shirts bowed over regulation paper,
rough haircuts hidden under watch caps, scars
concentration gouges deeper into

a forehead or cheek. What we share is this
little run of electricity each of us feels
as someone makes contact, a sharp image that lifts us
out of this place, though that's what they're all about—
the steel you grip so hard it aches a long time
in your half-open palms, held out like scales,

one bearing shame, the other desire.
And don't forget the scent of gasoline
and sweat, or the sudden commingling of
tobacco and sulphur that can slip through
any security, and get you,
wherever you are.

St. Mary's Blues

Nights, the hiss of breaking glass against
our steps, mingling with easy
slow dark voices—some laughter maybe,
piano sweet-talking the belly, then a sax.

Remember how our nights filled with those blues,
that sultry alto, our front stoop glittering,
the reeking men with bottles,
wanting to fill, wanting to break

and pour like no tomorrow. And those nights
could spill—a bottle knocked on a stair rail,
slicing up somebody's face, one voice gone
shrill, the others a murmur of quarrels

till sirens blew them away. A lull,
remember, then Lenny next door, gruff, garbled,
his boys shrieking, *No, Daddy, no, please.*
We'd pace, not knowing what to do but wait

five minutes, call the cops, those stiff shoes,
flashlights on the door the mother refuses
to open, while the boys sob through the cracks,
Don't, don't take him. All this, the next morning

Lenny would sweep onto newsprint, toss
in the trash, some pieces slivered but still held
by the label's glue as I was held to you
by a whiff strong as liquor not yet soaked

into wood. Heading for the shower,
we'd hear glass clatter in a metal bin,
Lenny mumbling to a Virgin Mary
propped against his fence. Then when his sons

came out he'd knuckle their crewcuts, straighten
their St. Mary's ties, begging their faces
for a grin. Some days I paced our rooms
as if the world were tilting and my weight

on one end could tip it, send us all over
the edge—you and me, and those stiff, red-eyed,
day-after men, Lenny hosing the stairs,
his two boys growing pudgy, padding themselves

with Milk Duds, packing away their rage till
I wanted to shake them, break the seal on
that bottle before it blew. One night—
remember? Sirens faded and the brawl

outside dissolved into one man's voice,
throaty and plaintive, sobbing into his hands
or the used tweed of somebody's shoulder.
October, orange moon, like some mix of

Tang and cheap vodka. That man dropped us
straight down, like the heart break wail of a sax,
his thick muffled voice on our doorstep,
crying *Sorry, sorry*. I let you in,

deeper than I ever had, my fingers
in your hair like the deaf alphabet
Lenny fumbled over his sons. What else
was there that night but sorry—sorry

that our loving doesn't change the world
outside, sorry that the man against
the streetlight swayed, rubbing his fists
in his eyes like a schoolboy, then stumbled off.

Sorry, I said to Mary, still propped
at the fence, and, Mother of Blues, with her
unflinching gaze she spoke to me. Cry, Girl,
she said, go on and let yourself loose.

Three Wishes

That was the winter the city hired two guys
to demolish by hand our neighbor's arsoned house—
chimney, foundation, beams on the second floor.
All January they worked with a teakettle whistling
on a trash fire, a boom box full of James Brown
"feeling good." I didn't, sitting in my coat

cheering through a fire-gouged hole in my wall,
seeing more house innards than I wanted, little slats
crumbling plaster, flimsy as an uncased brain or heart,
frog-slippery in the surgeon's hand. With crowbar
and Taj Mahal they'd grin, high-fiving each other
each time they brought a big chunk down.

That was the winter you sat in somebody's basement
on the floor, eyes shut, nodding *amen*
to the pale young preacher who kept declaring
spirit and flesh were at war. What am I, I turned
from the sink, threw a sponge at you—and our son,
what's he, lying rigid, awake in his bed

trying to save us from the fire that flares
whenever he shuts his eyes? You were stern and thin
that winter, nothing like the young man in the tree,
reaching shyly into my blouse for a cigarette.
The memory made you flinch as if I'd blown smoke
in your face, which was how our downstairs neighbor

said your brother looked—blown away, honey—
when he saw the house next door gutted, ours charred,
and drove off. Later he stared at his hands
explaining to me that he never knew how it felt
with a man his own strength, to dance, to stand
in the smoky bar, almost faint in his arms.

There was more to say than either of us could bear
as we sat on scaffolding stuck through my open wall,
blew our noses on paper towels. The guys pried
up pieces of linoleum, sailed them across the yard.
They hammered and chipped at chimney mortar
till they cracked a good hunk loose, slapped five,

shoved it down. The yard was all brick, charred
wood, shingles, stuffing from God knows where.
That night I sang as our son stared at ceiling
cracks. I closed my eyes, saw your brother
slow-dancing in the rubble, entwined with his friend,
then those two guys holding a charred window

they had jimmied loose. Let it fall, I wanted to say—
but to whom? And who do you ask what's happening,
will it be all right? If you're real, I dared something
over my head, make this light flash. But it didn't happen
that way, just because I thought I couldn't go on. You do,
my downstairs neighbor told me, with her cosmetic case

of pills to fine-tune her kinky head. You go on.
You even apologize for wanting to be spared,
she said one day, the dark roulette flash of her eyes
laughing at everything as our kids sailed
asbestos scraps through the gutter.
You got fire, what more do you want?

Forget Your Life

after Rumi

Plaster drips from the ceiling.
You close your eyes and think *skylight*.
All night you jackhammer through asphalt,
but in the morning the surface resumes unchanged
and people drive nonchalantly to work.
So what good is thinking about God
when it doesn't blow the tiles off the roof
or buckle the street, heaving up layers
of sandstone beneath the city?

Steam from the molten rocks of elementary
textbooks taught you how things squeeze
to a boil in the center of earth. You've been
squinting ever since, clenching your jaw,
at war with yourself, two deaf mutes
constantly jabbing. One of which proclaims,
God is Great! The other doesn't so much disagree
as think that's the trouble.

It takes a certain kind of violence
to wrench yourself free. A certain shock
to make you quit talking and give that helpless
shrug, the first step in a dance that turns
faster and faster. Even accountants get dizzy
and wad up their checks. Even philosophers
begin to laugh.

Don't be surprised to find yourself walking close
to the edge of a dock and suddenly tripping,
unable to keep your fists jammed in your pockets.

There's a whole school of ragged children
lined up on the riverbank. Look how heavy
the mistrustful ones are. They lift their feet
and drop straight down. Each day now,
I say this to myself: Forget your life.
Prayer is a different use of words, not these
frantic splashes demanding so much help no one can get near.

Don't go to work. Call in sick, or not
sick but desperate. You've been trying too hard
to unearth the perfect student, one who reads
so intently all her rough opinions leave her
like swine rushing over a cliff. Now, teach yourself.

Ladders and Ropes

"Music, by definition is not random,"
my student writes in freshman comp,
and I read while eerie sounds come up
from the basement: the cat strolling
on the old piano again with his beautiful
black feet, deliberating it seems, stepping
back, pausing, stepping forward up the scale.

Through the walls of my childhood I had no idea
why my sister's practice turned into scary dreams—
Mother with menacing nails, or our furniture
out on the street lurching on tracks like a horror
house ride, my sister's hands on the dark octaves
over and over as if if she stopped
something worse would happen.

I can close my eyes and still see her sway,
biting her lips, hours every day, weeping over
how hard it was to get the music right.
At dinner she'd shush me and go on
about not being good enough, or somebody else
being better, all the while stretching her fingers
on the table edge or the back of a chair

because the music was always too big, someone else's
she must strain for. *Not me,* I thought.
I didn't play a thing, but if I did, I'd wear
shades, blow the harp in our neighbor's band
like the shy girl who turned her back on everyone.
But when the music took hold, her whole body
flared, we could almost see the notes rippling

as she bent and wailed and forgot herself.
We'd forget her too—or not forget exactly,
but feel different, no longer wishing she'd turn,
or wondering why she slammed the door and the car
peeled out, left her on the sidewalk, mascara running
down her face. Now it was a bigger cry, one
with room for all of us, whatever we've lost.

Once I saw a woman sing the psalms of David like that,
the church bland and dreary, no place to recoup
a loss or make peace with traveling light.
When she got up, huge, shaped like a big-breasted
operatic hen from an old cartoon, I saw
it took every bit of her to sing that grief,
the death of a son conceived in fiery passion

that had already cost one man's life,
the terrible knowledge that all our regret can't
change what's done. The first time I saw my sister
really forget everything else in the room, she moved
so far into the music I had to close my eyes and listen
hard to the organ's swell, the ladders and ropes
of sound like rigging. I had to forgive her,

and trust, she was so intent on something
in the distance, steering us toward it.
Next morning we laughed at the headline—Little Lady
Makes Big Sound—and the reviewer's detailed notation
on how she pushed off and slid across the bench,
shimmied down to reach all the pedals and stops,
because by then we knew, when it's good it's

always too big, and that's why in the blues
the singer sometimes runs out of words,
why the psalmist cries, "A broken heart you will
not despise,"
           and that night when she kept her hand
on the keys and shut down the organ, there was such a long
dying of sound, we didn't see how far we had gone
into the silence.

The World Snow Posits

for Roy

1

This morning I went running six miles an hour
through the graveyard into another world
where snow falls—visible time, past and future.
Huge pines, swaying like sea plants in a tide
filled with white plankton, convinced me, by leaps
rather than logic, of heights above us where something
lives in an element too light for our lungs:
that other world snow always posits, though its code
is inscrutable, and when its veils disappear all we find
is the hard edge of this world, and a speech
without inflection in which these thoughts flicker out.

I'd been listening to your voice on the phone
suggesting that if no two are alike,
then difference is what we all share,
and any thought can swirl into its opposite,
like the word *random*, which you said
means, not "patternless," but having one
whose code hasn't been cracked.

Later, dozing at the window, I let snowflakes
drift through my mind—*snowfleck, snowflack,
snowflags* blowing off roofs and trees,
snowflock, flotsam melting on the pond,
and then that eerie foghorn blowing the years
till I fell back through snow flaring,
a car driving into its fury—the old fear
that because my father went off in snow
on a day when the lake was gray and all-absorbing,
only a slender white rail at the end of the road
keeps me from daring the same dissolution.

2

But the way your hand shakes,
it's as if my father were caught halfway between
body and soul in some torture of trembling, a galactic traveler
partially transported when the system breaks down.

You're stuck in a frozen face,
throat caught midswallow,
you with your seven languages, at a loss for words,
staring at frost patterns on the window

while in the next room,
loud enough for you to hear, my sister is saying
she didn't know what marriage meant, she hadn't read
the fine print—*sickness* and *worse*.

As if I could feel what a weakened body
does to the mind, I try not eating, and all day
growing dizzy remember last summer, that afternoon on the rocks,
overlooking the ocean, long before snow fell,

before anything external made them
treacherous—
how you tried to hold down your hand in a pocket,
then pressed it against your side as if the shake could be
smothered. A wave caught us unprepared

and we both nearly fell.
When the next one came you exaggerated the tremor,
shaking arms, legs, rolling your eyes till we broke down and
laughed, making our way to the car, arm in arm

like two stooges yipping and honking,
    a slapstick saint and his sidekick.
Is it always like this—against our will, in adversity,
        the spirit rises?

          I would have asked something else for you,
    some untried voluble ease. But that's not an option, is it—
in this world, where elements swirl and sometimes the gift is
        hunger and trembling.

3

Last night I tried to pray as sleep fell,
    silently covering the steps, and in that daze
        it seemed possible to collapse the long climb
and arrive instantly someplace without effort or stress,
      where hands don't shake, speech doesn't take
      so painfully long—

Remember how we'd laugh at dinner, singing old show tunes
    I knew half the words to, you knew the rest?
      Or there you are on your lawn chair reading
Tillich and Camus in the jungle. And here's one—
      you squatting beside a land-rover among children
        bunched dark and grinning around you.

But pain breaks speculation, and last summer driving home
    from those rocks, I used the road as an excuse to not look
      when you said every morning you struggled
as if knocking at a wall and sometimes you couldn't find
      the passage. It was easier in prison where the Spaniards
      shoved you into a cluster of Africans

who broke your fall, taught you the call and response
        you sang with them all night, unnerving your jailors—rhythms
            still clear in your mind despite your cacophonous hands,
        a language not written but tonal, shifting
            from blame to praise, dread to love—the kind of love
                nobody comes to till everything else is gone,

the way those men came to music made from their own bodies,
        clapping dense syncopations for dawn, dust-covered leaves,
            a lover's arms, the fierce dignity of their children,
        of lives good enough to die for. Which some of them did.
            And the rest? I asked in traffic, my hand
                gripping the wheel so tightly it was numb,

while you who are broken a different way,
        ran your finger across my white knuckles, telling me
            grief raises questions I try to answer too soon,
        not with my whole life, which is what saints learn
            is required when they sit all night, letting love fall
                in textures we have no language to conceive.

4

Two days without food and I go to the aquarium
where there are fish you can see right through,
fish thinner than you. This bright hypnotic flux
where so little matters, or else everything does—

as Ghandi or St. Francis would say—every word,
gesture, thought matters and constantly moves,
floats, darts through water, and two words
keep haunting me, *Let Go,* as if we could just sway

lightheaded between opulent tanks, calm
among sharks, while it snows outside,
nothing essential lost—is that possible,
all this trembling and nothing lost?

What the saints all tell you is *fast and pray.*
For what I'm not sure, but perhaps it's not
relief. Who can say what happens
when thoughts drift and words lose direction,

or how it is that *God* is not just outside,
an object addressed, but submerged,
raising bright fish in your mind,
as if all the while you thought you were looking—

just the opposite, some tide's been pulling you
out of every known thing
into that invisible world where all flags
surrender—as you told me you learned once

singing harmonies through the night in a language
where tone alters everything: how all the while
you thought you were locked-up in prison,
it was just the opposite, just the opposite.

At the Aquarium

Once a student told me she made love
to a night watchman beside this tank
expecting the liquid heat of passion

to lift them over all bounds. She woke
disillusioned and relieved, unable
to remember his name, as I've

forgotten hers, though I still think of them
lying just outside these tons of water
where sharks make their glaring rounds.

Even in the afternoon, I'm almost stunned
by flashlight fish from the sea's heaviest
depths, how they've grown radiant and fierce

under unfathomable pressure,
and I turn to penguins and otters,
ones who surface, make noise, whom we can

imagine embracing though they don't
have regular arms. Sometimes I imagine
a judgment in which our lives are revealed

clear as the bones of glass catfish.
Lionfish and carp—both would be stripped,
no hiding behind venom or beauty.

I'm not sure I want to know whether these
kissing fish are insatiably hungry
or filled with delight. I'd like to come out

tropical and bright, an extravagant
angel, incessant as sharks gliding the generous
buoyancy of paradise. When do I get to enter

like this diver, flippered and masked,
tumbling backward among fins, mouths,
the slow green sway where everything matters?

Into the Woods

Lord God, don't help me out by the clearing
where I know nothing of the stars and after
the first spin find all paths
look the same as the one I was sure
I could follow back reversing myself toward
the big safety light at the edge of the wood.

Compared to the even greater spin someone
has put on the earth, its enormous wobble,
I'm a little swirl, not moving at all, off
balance for an indeterminant half-life.

Dusk fades, and the forest turns
dark on dark, throwing its bristling
mystery against the sky. The whole night
is a door flung open. My down jacket
makes me brave, the zipper already broken
when I found it on the step of the Baptist
Youth Camp, left there three days
for someone to claim. Not something

the earth can just settle over
and obscure, I feel myself
take shape in this dark wood, glasses
shattered against a spruce.

After I cry and see how huge and sober
my breath has grown, maybe I will finally lose
sight of the great divorce of order and upheaval,
their joint custody, the way they've been passing
me back and forth my whole life.

Joining the Circus

Hadn't I gone to see clowns with bald heads, red noses?
I wanted to scream. Jumbo feet, huge collars,
the real version of what I drew at night
under the covers by flashlight in order to sleep,
to stop thinking about long black cars and holes in the ground,
and what I knew in my stomach was happening to my father's face.

But I saw how it would be
from the back seat of that car, my uncle's
limousine, driving home from the circus, jammed
in traffic on Mott Street. My eyes felt huge and stretched
watching disheveled men roll theirs and mutter,
then take wild staggering swings at invisible creatures.
One peed on our tire. Inside the car, my uncle
rolled and locked the windows by remote control.
Nobody said a word.

At least, nobody spoke to me.
My mother looked straight ahead. From the back,
my uncle could have been my father, except he never
turned and called me Squirt, or squeezed my knee
and made stupid faces.

What I found instead was the saddest man in the world,
a wilted flower in his coat, a tear tattooed on his cheek,
sweeping his shadow to miserable music. So didn't it
make sense now to find a whole street of miserable men
stumbling, not to laughter, but to laughter's other side—
horns and fists?

One lurched in and out, squeezing between bumpers and
grills. Red eyes, crew-cut cheeks. When he came
to our car, he cocked his head and stooped.
He pressed his hands against the glass of my window,
as if maybe he knew me from somewhere. Maybe I

was his face in an old mirror, or he was mine.
His breath clouded the glass. I tried to wipe it away,
but he kept moving his tongue inside his mouth as if I
should be able to know how it feels.

I put my hand on the glass to match his.
My uncle let the car roll, then slammed the brakes
and he slid away. But he had come. Just as he did
at night when I drew under the covers.
Because that's what people do after they die.
And I will too. Sooner or later, before or after,
one day I will move among cars, looking through rain-
smeared windows, then place my palms on the glass,
gathering the sound of horns, the disconnected
waving of fists, the terrible love
you have to have nothing to feel.

Three Deaths

Last autumn, tensed for winter, I was sealing up
windows, wrapping shrubs in burlap. I never thought of spring,
never considered putting those cold bulbs in the ground.

But outside the halfway house, under moonlight,
my nephew, possessed by growing delusions, carefully sowed what
resembled to him shrunken heads, the dark insides of a scream.

And my friend, in brief remission, waved me away
with my solemn worry while she kneeled in the rain cold
garden, emaciated, hairless, white as bone. *It's grim enough,*
she hissed, trying to whistle.

November, December, January, she wrote letters
about accepting what we're given. *This isn't passivity,*
she said. *I've come to see I've been given a lot.*

February, my nephew's garbled note read,
where I'm going knives don't exist, pianos and doors
will not rise up against me: *Rejoice, my friends.*

But now it is March, and the graveyard is full of these
trumpets and flares. I don't bother to read the stones
because this month every one is my father's, whose voice
I try to remember and can't.

He didn't leave me a single word, though I did hear him laugh.
I have pictures of him leaning on a fence
like a mirthful grasshopper chewing tobacco:

Busy busy busy, he seems to chide the diligent ants,
my father, who when he knew he would die, licked the flap
of a manilla envelope bearing my name in which he had placed

such strange advice: four pennies hammered into a tea set,
a monkey carved out of peach pit, assorted puzzles, key rings,
a whistle shaped like a tiny violin.

About the Author

BETSY SHOLL grew up in Brick Town, New Jersey. She earned degrees from Bucknell University, the University of Rochester, and Vermont College. Her previous books are *Changing Faces*, *Appalachian Winter*, and *Rooms Overhead*. She was the 1991 winner of the Maine Arts Commission chapbook competition, and a recipient of an Individual Artists Fellowship from the Maine Arts Commission. She lives with her family in Portland, Maine and teaches at the University of Southern Maine. *The Red Line* was selected by Ronald Wallace as the winner of the 1991 Associated Writing Programs' award series in poetry.

Pitt Poetry Series

Ed Ochester, General Editor